Crossroads

A Monologue Collection

To Nathaniel + Bea,
we so enjoy spending time
with you + your kids!
God bless

love,
Aunt Carla

Carla Friesen-Martin

AT THE CROSSROADS
Copyright © 2018 by Carla Friesen-Martin

Printed in Canada

ISBN: 978-1-4866-1730-2

Word Alive Press
131 Cordite Road, Winnipeg, MB R3W 1S1
www.wordalivepress.ca

RECYCLED
Paper made from
recycled material
FSC® C103567

Cataloguing in Publication may be obtained through Library and Archives Canada

This book is dedicated with much love to
Glen, Mikaela, and Samantha.

Acknowledgments

This monologue collection is the culmination of more than twenty years of exploring the lives of people in the Bible through writing and drama. I'm grateful to the past and present pastors of the Ministerial Association of Williams Lake, and to the Women's Ministries groups of Calvary Church and the Williams Lake Evangelical Free Church for their encouragement to write, and opportunities to present, many of these monologues.

Many thanks to Marina and the team at Word Alive Press for guiding me through the process of making this book a reality, and to my aunt, Margaret Friesen, who was also instrumental in making this possible. Thanks, too, to my brother, Kevin Friesen, for the photo shoot.

Most of all, my deepest thanks to my husband, Glen, for your love, support, and encouragement, and for your gentle nudges to take this plunge. And to Mikaela and Samantha for putting up with your mother showing up in public wearing funny costumes, and still being willing to be seen with me.

Contents

Introduction

One of the greatest gifts my parents gave me was the Bible. I still remember the day they bought me my very own, just about as soon as they thought I'd be able to read it for myself. Even before that, Bible stories had always been a part of my life.

Having those stories and truths ingrained in me has been a tremendous gift. However, the downside to being steeped in the Bible from day one, if there is a downside, is that you start to read every story with the ending in mind. And when you do that, the people in the Bible become characters—not real people, but people who are qualitatively different than you or me.

I don't know about you, but I'm no epic hero. I'm not Moses commanding the Red Sea to part or Mary being hand-picked to carry the Messiah. I've never had superhuman strength or slain a giant with a slingshot. (If you've ever seen me try to do a chin-up or throw a baseball, you just know that ain't gonna happen.)

With familiarity came the sense that while I could learn lessons from the characters in the Bible, I could never really identify with them, because, cultural differences aside, they're not quite like the rest of us.

Writing these pieces changed my view on that. It started as simply a way to view a few familiar stories in a new way, to imagine what the characters' stories looked like from their perspectives, while staying as true as I could to the biblical text.

When I started putting together the larger collection, it struck me that there was a common thread: each of the people whose stories I was trying to tell were standing at a crossroads. Faced with a challenge or crisis of faith, each one had to make a decision—to obey God or turn away from him, to trust God or give in to fear, to accept God's sovereignty, even when they didn't understand him, or keep trying to call the shots themselves.

Those are moments with which I can identify. I suspect you can, too.

The more I wrote, the more it occurred to me that each of these characters was a real person. (Well, except Celeste. But that piece was too much fun to leave out.) None of them knew how their stories were going to end when they stood at the crossroads, and they didn't know how their choices would become part of God's greater story of redemption. But each one faced moments when God called them to choose the path of faith, of trust—just like when God calls you and me to make decisions that often seem insignificant, but also sometimes overwhelming. We have all at times found ourselves standing at a crossroads.

Some of the pieces in this collection depict people looking back on the decisions they've made. Others stand on the verge of taking a leap of faith, and their stories may leave the audience guessing as to which choice they will make.

My prayer is that as you prepare and present these pieces, you and your audience will connect in a new way with real people from the Bible. May you be encouraged and strengthened by their stories when you find yourself standing at a crossroads.

Not What I Had Planned

Mary

Cast: 1 female
Props: None

IT WAS NOTHING LIKE I'D PLANNED.

Growing up in Nazareth, my life was pretty much the same as my friends'. We spent our days learning to keep house and look after children. We worshiped at the synagogue and learned about our heritage as God's chosen people. Our plans were simple: to live in Nazareth, have homes and families of our own, and, God willing, see the coming of the Messiah, the promised one.

Everything was going according to plan. When I turned fifteen, my parents told me I was to be engaged to Joseph. I didn't know him well, since a man and woman aren't allowed to talk to each other in public. But I knew all about him. I knew he was a carpenter, like his father—a very good one. I knew he made toys from leftover bits of wood for children who came by his shop. I knew that he was a good man, even though he wasn't rich or influential, and I was honoured by the match.

Then all my plans fell apart. One day, a day just like any other, I was alone in my parents' house, making bread, when an angel appeared.

You don't believe me, do you? I'm not surprised. Nobody else did. How could I really explain to anybody what it's like to see an angel, or to know in my heart that he was real? But I knew. I knew, because around here a girl grows up obeying her parents. As a woman, she obeys her husband. All through her life, she learns to obey the Law. I knew this vision—this angel—had come from God because when he told me I'd been chosen by God to bear his son, I knew I could say no. Only God is powerful enough to risk giving us a choice in something so big and important.

Poor Joseph. This definitely wasn't what he'd planned. He might not have had one of the best seats at the front of the synagogue, but people respected him. At least they did until I, the woman he'd chosen for his wife, publicly humiliated him.

Under our Law, he could have had me stoned to death for adultery, and nobody would have blamed him. But instead he decided to break off our engagement quietly, for my sake, until God's angel came and spoke to him, too. He told Joseph, in a dream, that this child was God's own Son, and that we were part of a much greater plan than anything we'd ever imagined for ourselves.

And so we were married. People whispered and pointed fingers, but we loved making our home and looked forward to raising our son there.

Suddenly our plans fell apart again. The Roman emperor decided to take a census of his whole empire. Joseph, along with every other man in Israel, was ordered to return to his ancestral hometown to register for taxation.

With the baby's birth so near, I was hardly in any condition to travel. But Joseph and I decided that the journey to Bethlehem, a place where nobody knew us, would be a chance to start fresh. In Bethlehem, we could raise our son away from pointing fingers and whispered insults. And so we packed whatever we could, said goodbye to our families, and started on the journey.

By the time we arrived in Bethlehem, after days of travel by foot and donkey, my labour pains started. Throngs of people had arrived ahead of us. Finding a room in such a small village would have been hard at the best of times. Now it was impossible. All anyone could offer us was a stable. It was no more than a cave, but at least it was a roof over our heads. And it was there that our son was born.

Before we could even get settled in Bethlehem, our plans fell apart yet again. Another angel appeared to Joseph in a dream, warning him that King Herod knew about Jesus and was trying to kill him. I mean, there we were, practically in the shadow of Herod's fortress, and he was looking for us. Joseph woke me up, and we left that night, running for our lives to Egypt.

It wasn't until Herod died that it was finally safe for us to return home. As Jesus grew up in Nazareth, Joseph and I watched him closely, wondering what this Messiah would be. Everybody had plans for the Messiah—mainly plans for him to build up an army and drive the Romans out of Israel. But as a child, Jesus was more of a dreamer, not one of the boys who liked to play soldier or scrap it out in the streets.

When he was older, Jesus started talking about a new kind of kingdom, one that wasn't based on political power or geography. He amazed us with the authority with which he spoke and the miracles he performed. His teachings seemed to take all our beliefs and stand them on their heads, yet they made us feel like we were really understanding them for the first time.

Bit by bit, I found myself believing that Jesus really was the Messiah, God's chosen one, that God's plan was really being carried out through my son.

And then, all of a sudden, it seemed that even God's plans fell apart. As Jesus travelled around, preaching about God's new kingdom, he made plenty of enemies. One Passover night, a crowd led by the chief priests and elders arrested Jesus and tried him, and the very next day they executed him. I'll never forget standing at the foot of the cross on which they'd nailed my son, crying out to God, "Surely this wasn't what you planned!"

I should have known that God's plans never work the way I picture them. Two days after he died, I heard that Jesus was alive again, and then I saw him myself. Oh, you can try and explain that one away. But I know. When they took Jesus down from the cross, and I held his broken body, there was no denying that he was dead. Don't think I didn't try. And when I saw him alive again, I knew my son. And it was then I knew that, all his life, I'd also been learning to know God.

The prophets said that my son would be called Emmanuel, "God with us." For generations, we'd tried to speed his coming by obeying the Law, trying to keep ourselves pure. We'd hoped that God would come to meet us through our rituals and festivals. Don't get me wrong—those things are all fine and good. They remind us who God is, and who we are in relation to him. But God doesn't come to us according to our plans or in the ways we expect. Emmanuel, "God with us," didn't come as a prince or a warrior, but as one who would be vulnerable and broken, so that we can know his presence when we're at our most vulnerable and broken.

Of all people, I should know. Emmanuel didn't come to me according to any of my plans. My son, Jesus, was born in a stable, surrounded by the smell of animals and unwashed people. And to everyone around us, I was nothing but a sinner and an outcast. It was the last place anyone expected to find the Messiah. And yet it was then and there that I held God in my arms.

All I Have to Offer

Joseph

Scripture: Matthew 1:18–24
Cast: 1 male
Props: Simple wooden workbench or table
Stool
Piece of wood
Mallet and chisel or planing tool

(Scene opens with Joseph working at his carpenter's bench, planing or hammering. He's upset; it shows in the way he attacks the wood. Frustrated, he throws down his tools and sits on a stool, burying his head in his hands. Finally, he looks up.)

LORD, HELP ME. I DON'T KNOW WHAT TO DO.

You know, I had it all figured out before you stepped in. A quiet divorce. Mary's life is spared; I salvage what's left of my reputation and get on with my life. But then you send me an angel who tells me I'm supposed to marry her, even though she's pregnant with a child who's not mine. What am I supposed to say to an angel? "Sorry. I had other plans"?

I suppose you think sending an angel to tell me what to do should make this easy. But it doesn't! Mary's on her way back from her cousin's place. She'll be here any day, and I need to give her an answer. I know what you want me to do, but it's still hard!

I'll never forget how she looked when she told me she was pregnant, that the child is the Messiah, conceived by the

Holy Spirit. She looked so scared, but brave, too. Accepting. Needing me to believe her.

I didn't know what to think. I mean, come on. The Holy Spirit? I was supposed to buy that? That was crazy! I needed time to think, to figure out what to do. I guess she'd seen that coming. She'd already made plans to visit her cousin near Jerusalem, to buy me some time.

Most people would just charge her with adultery and let her be stoned. But I can't let them kill her just for the sake of my pride. Don't get me wrong. I'm angry. Furious, actually. I just don't know who I'm angrier at—her, or you.

Lord, it hurts. All my life, I've tried to honour you. To do the right thing. And now, if I do what you tell me, I'll be a laughingstock. I know what people will say: that I couldn't keep my hands off her, or that she was unfaithful, or just plain crazy.

Why wouldn't they? That's what I thought when she told me about that whole Holy Spirit thing. Still, it isn't like Mary to lie. So why would she say it?

And then it hit me. Sometimes even the most honest people can be pushed to do or say desperate things if... I mean, I knew the child wasn't mine, and she swore she'd been faithful. So what if... I mean, there are some men who... *(Angry, he can't bring himself to say it outright)* Not that I wanted it to be true, but it was the only thing that made sense.

So I figured divorce was the answer. I couldn't make people stop gossiping or pointing fingers, and I couldn't undo what happened to Mary. But at least I could spare her from a trial, or stoning.

And now you send me an angel, after months of agonizing. Don't get me wrong. It helps to know Mary was telling the truth, that this child is really yours. But I'm still struggling.

Maybe it *is* my pride. If I take Mary as my wife, it'll be like I'm admitting the child's really mine. Well, so be it. Let people say what they want. If Mary can stand it, so can I.

But what about the child? Even if he's yours, I need to be a real father to him. I don't want to raise a child—any child—at arm's length. And there'll be enough people whispering and pointing fingers. He'll need all the love and acceptance he can get from me. I'll never forget he's yours, but he'll have to be mine, too. I don't know any other way.

If we're going to do this, Lord, there's one more thing. I don't feel like I have what it takes to raise a Messiah. I mean, look at this place. I'm a carpenter, not a king. I don't have a fancy education or connections. It's hard enough just to keep food on the table and a roof over our heads. What can I possibly offer the Messiah?

Still, I guess great leaders don't always start off in palaces. Gideon was a farmer. And David was a shepherd. All he had to work with was a sling and stones.

(Picking up his discarded tools) I don't have a lot to offer, but I'll give him what I have. I'll be a father to him, and a husband to his mother. I'll love them and provide for them and protect them as best I can. I'll teach him all I know—not just about carpentry but about serving you.

(Standing up and brushing the woodchips off himself) All right, Lord, I'll do it. I, Joseph son of David, your servant, offer you myself. I'll be a father to your child. I'll look after him the best I can, and trust you to deal with the rest.

And now, if you don't mind, I've got to get to work. I've got a wedding gift to make for my wife. And a cradle for our son.

Plans and Preparations

Celeste, an angel

Cast: 1 female
Props: Clipboard

(Celeste enters carrying clipboard, nervously composing herself. Rather than a flowing gown, she wears a white business suit, or skirt and blouse, with wings.)

WOW, FIRST DAY ON THE NEW JOB. AM I EVER NERVOUS! THIS IS A big promotion. Okay, self, calm down. Take a deep breath... Here he comes!

(Saluting) Angel Celeste reporting for duty, sir!

(Gushing) Before we get started, I'd just like to say how thrilled I am to have been chosen to be your personal assistant, sir. Especially now that you're preparing for your big mission. The Son of God, going down to earth... this is really big! I mean, when the job was posted, I figured for sure it'd go to Gabriel or Michael, or at least one of the seraphim. I guess what I'm trying to say is, thanks for choosing me. I won't let you down, sir!

(Brought up short) That soon? Oh, indeed! Let's get started then.

Actually, sir, to that end, I've taken the liberty of jotting down a few thoughts on the arrangements for your trip. You know, take some of the pressure off you. I know you've got a lot on your plate right now...

(Embarrassed) Well, yes, I guess omnipotence does come in handy there.

(Brightening) Oh... you'd like to hear them? Okay. Well, first off, we need to give careful thought as to where you'll be making your big entrance. You know what they say: "Location, location, location!" I know you did some pretty spectacular work at Mount Sinai in Moses' time—fire and smoke, thunder and lightning, earthquakes—great special effects! But according to my marketing research, there aren't many people there now other than the odd nomad and his sheep. So I was thinking... picture it, sir... Rome! It's the capital of the biggest empire on earth, and I've taken the liberty of booking the amphitheatre. It's huge! Seats thousands. And with your connections, we could probably even get the Emperor to attend!

Judea? *(Dubiously)* Well, I guess that could work... I know you've been working with people in the area for a long time. Of course, you must mean Jerusalem. You could appear at the temple. It's on top of a hill—great sight lines and publicity...

No, I can't say I've ever heard of Bethlehem. Is it one of those new luxury cities the Romans have been building? *(Dryly)* A farming village. Population eighty-six. Well, I guess the census will inflate our numbers somewhat. *(Brightening)* All right. Bethlehem it is.

Perhaps we should move along. *(Consults list)* Ah, yes. Wardrobe! We both know how important it is to create a good first impression. So I took a look around our wardrobe department for ideas and found some stunning robes in gold and silver. I thought we could have something made up for you in those fabrics, add some jasper and carnelian detailing on the yoke, a few bolts of lightning on the shoulders... No, I didn't see any boxes marked "swaddling clothes," but if you give me your size, I'm sure we could have some made up... Oh? They'll be provided on arrival? Great! *(Suddenly confused, as a thought dawns)* But then, how will you...? *(Embarrassed)* On second thought, never mind. I'll just check that off the list for now.

Next item: mode of transportation. We have several options here. You could just appear out of nowhere—BAM!—but I think we need something with a little more pizzazz. You could float down on a bank of clouds. Cumulus nimbus is always very dramatic. Or we could polish up that old staircase from heaven. Personally, though, I've always been partial to the chariot of fire. Picture it, sir: swooping down out of the sky with horses and wheels ablaze, followed by a company of angels with swords drawn and trumpets blaring. Very impressive!... Um, I'm not familiar with that mode of travel. What, exactly, is "in utero"?... *(Aghast)* Oh! Seriously? Is that really necessary?

So what you're saying is that you're going to earth as a baby? A human baby? With all due respect, sir, have you *seen* what babies do?... Well, yes, I'm aware that you designed them. *(Chastened)* Yes... I'm sorry, sir, no disrespect intended.

Well, that certainly puts things in a whole new light. If you're going down as a human and planning to stay a while, we'll have to assemble an away team. After all, earth isn't the cleanest or safest place. You'll need a security officer, and definitely a medical officer. And it might be a good idea to take along a science officer and collect samples while you're down there...

You've already selected leaders for the away team? Excellent. And they are...? But, sir, don't you think that a carpenter and a teenaged girl seem a little, well, underqualified?... Oh, you already have twelve more lined up for later in the mission? Excellent! Could I get their names and positions for my records? Let's start with the business manager... How do you spell "Iscariot"? Never mind. I'll get their names later from personnel.

Just a couple more things left on the list. Since you're planning to make a rather inauspicious entrance, a good publicity strategy becomes all the more important. What plans did you have, sir? *(Nods approvingly)* A star is good... and an angel choir. I'm liking the sound of that. They could perform at Herod's palace. All the movers and shakers will be there... But, sir, we want to get the attention of people of influence. Nobody's going to listen to shepherds. People don't like them. They're rough and dirty and, just between you and me, they smell funny... *(Resigned)* Right. Shepherds it is.

Dare I ask what you had in mind for accommodations when you arrive? *(Writing and muttering)* A stable and a manger. *(Putting down clipboard)* Permission to speak freely, sir? It's just that this is all very different from what I pictured when I first took this job. Has there been a change in plans? Did I miss the email?

I just don't understand. You're the Almighty. Ever since you created these people, the vast majority of them have turned their backs on you. I thought this was all about bringing them back in line. Hitting 'em with the might and the majesty, the glitz and the glory. Reminding them who they're dealing with here. You can't just show up down there as a baby! You'll be vulnerable, defenceless. I mean, what do you think will happen to you if you go down there as one of them?

Crucified?! But, sir, why? Why can't you just do what you need to do from up here?

Sure, I know the meaning of the word "Emmanuel." We covered that in basic training. It means "God with us." *(Starting to dawn)* Oh! See, I always thought that just meant you were on their side. From up here. You know, like how you used to help Israel win battles... Well, yeah, you always said you created people to have a relationship with you. But I didn't realize you meant to go down there as one of them, walking through everything they go through, right there beside them... *(it's all coming clear now)* to draw them back into a relationship with you. To reach out directly, physically even, to the ones who've turned their backs on you.

But, sir, if they're just going to crucify you, doesn't that mean your plan won't work?... So what you're saying is that the only way to show them the best of your forgiveness and love for them is to let them do their worst to you.

(Shakes head) But, sir, then what do you need me for?... Oh, come on! You're... well, you're *God*. How could I possibly strengthen you? Although if you're going to be human, too, I guess you'll need strength and encouragement sometimes. All right. I'll do it, sir. Whatever happens—pain, hunger, rejection—I'll be there. You can count on me.

I know it's almost time for you to go. But before you do, I'd just like to say one last thing—because you may not hear it much when you're down there. Thank you, sir. For what you're doing. And for calling me to be a part of it. It's a privilege and a blessing to serve you.

(While turning to exit stage, regards paper on clipboard for a moment as if to make a note. Then takes paper off clipboard, balls it up, and throws it away.)

Good Friday

Mary Magdalene

Scripture: John 19:30
Cast: 1 female
Props: None

IT'S FINISHED.

Oh, God, it *is* finished. How could you let it end this way?

All along, some part of me's been thinking, "Any time now." Somehow, even after they'd nailed Jesus to that cross, you could have swooped down or sent your angels, or something, and everybody would see your kingdom come, just like he said it would.

But now it's all finished.

Jesus is dead. There's no kingdom. No Jesus. Already most of his disciples have taken off. How long before the rest of us do, too? Is this it? Is this the end of everything Jesus taught or did or promised?

If it is, then what was Jesus? A blasphemer or fraud? I can't believe that. Not after everything I've seen. So, what then? A dreamer? Please, God, he had to have been more than that.

Who was Jesus to me? He was my salvation. He was the one who saw me when everyone else only saw a crazy woman, full of demons. He was the one who touched me when nobody else would, who freed me when nobody else could.

Jesus was my friend. My teacher. My example and my safe place. Most of all, he was truth. When I heard echoes of the demons' whispers, his voice shut them up and sent them packing. Jesus' truth unmasked their lies and took away their power.

But now he's gone. And if Jesus isn't here, if he's not alive, then all I really have is me. *My* memories of what he said. *My* ability to understand it. My *own* strength to fight the lies and live the truth. And that's not enough.

I always thought truth was found in thoughts and words and ideas. But words and ideas have their limits. In walking with Jesus, I learned that truth is a person. Truth is God, and through Jesus I could walk and talk and interact with truth. Truth became not just something to try to grasp with my own ability, but a relationship in which truth worked in me and drew me to himself.

But now I'm on my own.

It is finished.

Easter Sunday

Mary Magdalene

Scripture: Mark 16:1–8, John 20:10–18
Cast: 1 female
Props: None

IT WAS THE FINAL INSULT: AN EMPTY TOMB.

Like they hadn't already done enough. They'd taken away our friend, our Messiah—our hope. They'd arrested him, beaten him, killed him like a criminal. And left us shattered.

At least we had one thing left, one last thing we could do to show our love for Jesus. So this morning, my friends and I bought spices and went to look after Jesus' body. It was our way of saying goodbye. We needed to know that the last hands that touched him would do it with respect, and out of love.

But when we got there, the tomb was empty. Jesus' body was gone. They couldn't even leave us that. They'd already killed him. What now?

So we told Simon Peter and John. They came to the tomb to see for themselves, but they couldn't figure it out, either. They saw the cloths he'd been wrapped in, and John said something about how Jesus had said he'd rise from the dead, but it was all so confusing.

After they left, I stayed behind. It was all too much— the grief and pain of everything that had happened were overwhelming and all I could do was cry until, finally, I decided to look into the tomb for myself.

When I stuck my head in, there were two men sitting there—angels, they must have been, but we didn't figure that out until later—sitting right where Jesus' body had been.

I had no idea where they'd come from—Peter and John hadn't said anything about them—and they asked me, "Woman, why are you crying?"[1]

I told them, "They've taken my Lord away, and I don't know where they have put him."[2]

Seeing them there shook me and I didn't know what else to say, so I backed out of the tomb. As I was turning around, I saw another man—the gardener, I guessed—and he asked me the same question: "Woman, why are you crying? Who is it you are looking for?"[3]

Again, I had to plead, "Sir, if you have carried him away, tell me where you have put him, and I will get him."[4]

And then I heard my name: "Mary."

I looked up to see that it wasn't the gardener—not a stranger at all, but Jesus. Alive!

The next hours were a blur. After the rush of going and telling everybody, of the hugs and tears and amazement, only now do I have time to think about what happened in the garden. When it was just Jesus and me. Time to think about what Jesus said... and what he didn't say.

When I was a little girl, hurt and crying, my mother often told me to stop crying and dry my eyes. To get over whatever had hurt me or scared me and move on.

Jesus never said that. He asked me, "Why are you crying?" and then he let me answer. He didn't interrupt me or tell me to dry my eyes, or say it didn't matter anymore because he was alive. He listened. Jesus accepted me, my tears, my grief. Instead of brushing all that away, he stepped into my darkest moment, shared it with me, and invited me to name it. And then he transformed it.

In one word, "Mary," he told me that he knew me and invited me to know him, too—risen and alive. He transformed the tomb from the final insult, the final word, into a beginning. In a place reserved for death, Jesus was life.

Losing Jesus, first when he died and then by finding an empty tomb, I doubt I'll ever forget how that felt. But Jesus met me there—my living friend, my risen Saviour. And because of that, my deepest grief has become my greatest joy.

ᴏake this ᴄup

The Apostle John

Scripture: Mark 14:23–25, 1 Corinthians 11:23–26
Cast: 1 male
Props: Table and stool
Loaf of bread
Goblet
Jug with enough grape juice to fill goblet

(A small table stands centre stage, with a stool beside it. A loaf of bread, a simple goblet, and a jug with enough grape juice to fill the goblet are on the table. The apostle John enters, sits on stool, and picks up goblet. He holds it for a while, examining it, then holds it up and addresses the audience.)

Just a cup. The kind you use every day without thinking about it. A simple cup, and yet so full of meaning.

The cup has always fascinated me. Long ago, David sang, "You prepare a table before me in the presence of my enemies. You anoint my head with oil; my cup overflows."[5] For him, the cup was full of God's blessings, poured out to overflowing.

Other times, though, the cup was full of God's anger—like when God told the prophet Jeremiah, "Take from my hand this cup filled with the wine of my wrath and make all the nations to whom I send you drink it. When they drink it, they will stagger and go mad because of the sword I will send among them."[6]

Sometimes, when I was a boy, just seeing a cup sitting on a table or shelf would make me shudder. Because the cup of wrath wasn't just for our enemies. Time and again, Israel has had to drink from that cup, too, when we've turned our backs on God. For centuries, we needed the blood of innocent animals to cover up our sins every day, so that God would hold back that cup from us.

That's why Passover's such a special day. At Passover, instead of the cup of his wrath, God offers us four cups of his mercy. The cup of sanctification, to remind us how God promised to rescue us from slavery in Egypt. The cup of plagues, reminding us of the plagues God used to deliver us. The cup of blessing, reminding us of the blood of a lamb who saved us from death. And the cup of praise, to thank God for taking us to be his own people.

Every Passover, for all my life, I raised those cups, drinking in their full meaning. Or so I thought, until the Passover when Jesus was arrested.

It was in Jerusalem. We knew there was trouble. For months, Jesus' enemies had been watching for any excuse to have him arrested. And all week, crowds had been following him, hoping to see him make some big move against the Romans. But the upper room, where we'd met for the Passover meal, was quiet, a safe place away from the crowds and threat of arrest.

Like every other year, we told the story of the first Passover and our people's amazing escape from Egypt. We ate the bitter herbs of slavery and tasted the salt of Israel's tears. We drank cups of wine to remember God's promises and faithfulness, and we ate the lamb that had been sacrificed for us.

But when it was time for the cup of blessing, the cup of redemption, Jesus caught us all off-guard. Instead of pouring wine into each of our cups, he only filled his own and held it out to us. And then, instead of the usual prayer, he said,

"Drink from it, all of you. This cup is the new covenant in my blood, which is poured out for you."[7]

We thought he'd gone crazy! For those of us who were married, those were the words we'd said in our engagement ceremonies. By offering the cup, we were offering our lives: "This cup is a new covenant in my blood, which I offer to you." I can still remember the excitement—and terror!—of saying those words, the agony of waiting for an answer and the relief and amazement when the woman I loved took the cup and drank, promising her life to me.

And now here was Jesus, making that same offer, waiting for our answers. One by one, we took the cup and drank, knowing that once we did we wouldn't just be following Jesus anymore, but promising him our lives in return for his. No matter what.

I don't think any of us realized just how soon that promise would be put to the test.

After supper, we walked through the dark streets to Gethsemane. Nothing unusual there. The garden on the Mount of Olives was Jesus' favourite place to get away from the city.

All the way there, Jesus was quiet, like he was lost someplace inside himself. He told everybody else to stay near the entrance to the garden and asked Peter, James, and me to walk further with him. We had no idea what was going on, but I could see he was shaking.

When we got to a terrace that looked across to the city, Jesus told us to wait there and keep watch. *(Ironically)* Keep watch. We tried. We really did. But the food and wine were making us sleepy and pretty soon our eyes fell shut. It seemed like, in a dream, I could hear Jesus praying, begging God, "Father, my Father, please take this cup away from me. But if it's not possible for this cup to be taken away unless I drink it, let your will be done."

Father, take this cup. This cup... those words kept coming back to me through everything that happened next—through watching Jesus get arrested and tried, seeing him beaten and dying on a cross. What was the cup that God refused to take away? Was it the cup of God's wrath? But why would God pour out so much suffering and punishment on Jesus, who'd seemed chosen and blessed by God? It made no sense!

Those questions hurt almost as much as losing the friend I loved most—until the morning the women came running to tell us that the tomb was empty. Until Jesus appeared himself and showed us the scars on his hands and feet, explaining that he'd had to die so that he could be the sacrifice to end all sacrifices.

Then I understood. Jesus, God's chosen One, drank the cup that should have been ours, the cup of God's wrath, and in its place he offered us a new cup of blessing and redemption— the cup of a new covenant, a new relationship with God.

"Take this cup." I remember how easy that seemed before we knew what it really meant. When we thought Jesus' kingdom meant earthly glory and power.

My own mother once came to Jesus, asking him to promise that my brother and I would sit at his right and left hands in his kingdom—the positions of the greatest power and privilege. Instead of answering her, Jesus looked at us and asked, "Can you drink the cup I am going to drink?"[8] We thought, "Of course we can!" I'll never forget the sadness in Jesus' eyes when he told us, "You will indeed drink from my cup."[9]

Now I understand what that meant. It's the cup of his suffering. The cup of hardship and persecution and rejection. But now it's also the cup of redemption and blessing. It's the promise that if we accept *this* cup, we'll never have to taste the cup of God's wrath, because Jesus already drank it for us.

(John picks up the cup and fills it with wine/juice from the jug)
Jesus offered us the cup of blessing, the new covenant in his

blood. He offered us his life, if we'll bind our lives to his. For some of you, this cup is an invitation to celebrate, again, the gift you've received. To the rest of you, it's an invitation to trade the cup of God's wrath for the cup of redemption and blessing. For each of us, Christ fills the cup of blessing to over-flowing *(holding cup out)*, holds it out, and invites us: "Come. Take this cup."

7

Forgiven

The Woman Who Washed Jesus' Feet

Scripture: Luke 7:36–50
Cast: 1 female
Props: None

*(Woman walks to centre stage. She is grim as
she addresses the audience.)*

THIS IS THE DARKEST DAY OF OUR LIVES. WE HAVE NO TEARS LEFT. The heat and dust burned those dry hours ago. You'd think the sun could show some mercy. But mercy's the last thing you'll find at the place they call "the Skull."

A few of us huddle together, a small island in this sea of people who've come to watch men die. They watch one man in particular. The King of the Jews, they call him—our king whose hands drip blood, who fights for every breath. This is what they've come to see.

But none of them see his eyes—neither the pain nor the love as he looks down at his mother standing beside me. Her eyes are dry. But her hand, clinging to mine, shakes and grips me tighter, knowing it can't wipe the blood from his face or pull the spikes from his wrists. Instead her gaze offers him the comfort that her hands can't, to tell him she loves him. And to say goodbye.

Goodbye. Not just to Jesus, but to all the hopes we had of a new kingdom of love and justice and peace. *(Angrily)* Okay, maybe the sceptics were right. Maybe Jesus couldn't deliver on his promises. Still, you couldn't listen to Jesus and not believe him. He was so different from the priests and the Pharisees. They love to strut around, reminding us how important they are. But Jesus made us feel like we were important to him. And to God.

Everybody talked about Jesus—in the markets, in the city gates, even on their way to the synagogue. Not that they'd ever talk to me. People usually stopped talking when I walked by, pretended I wasn't even there, or snarled insults that I won't bother to repeat. Of course, those people never had to sell themselves for the price of their next bite of bread.

Even I couldn't miss hearing about Jesus; he was so controversial. Some people called him "rabbi"; others, "blasphemer." Some even said he was in league with Satan himself. *(Dismissively)* Whatever. All I cared was that wherever Jesus was, there'd be a crowd. And crowds were good for business.

So when Jesus came to town, I was there, too. At first I didn't pay any attention to him. I needed customers, not another preacher throwing my filth in my face. But as I worked the crowd, Jesus' words seemed to follow me, as if he were talking just to me. And when I finally started to listen, I realized that his words weren't accusing. He didn't condemn me for breaking the Law every day to fill my stomach, the way others broke bread to fill theirs. Instead his words told me that I was—get this—happy.

(Sarcastic) Happy? Happy because nobody would be seen in public with me, even though I'd do for a few minutes in a dark alley? *(Softening)* No. Happy, because I was poor and hungry. Happy—blessed, even—because I knew my pain by name. And for the first time in my life, somebody told me that God did, too.

That's why I had to see Jesus when I heard he was going to Simon's house, away from the crowds. Now, you have to understand how desperate I was to even think of setting foot in the home of a Pharisee, a man whose entire life revolved around keeping himself pure. But I couldn't forget Jesus or what he'd said. The darkness of my life was swallowing me up, and Jesus was the only way out that I could see. If I grabbed on to him, I didn't know whether he'd hold on to me and pull me out of that pit or simply let go. But I had to find out.

I didn't have anything to offer Jesus, except my only treasure—a bottle of perfume that had been in my mother's dowry, and her mother's before her. It was the only shred of evidence I had left that I, too, had once had a respectable life. I doubted Jesus could accept somebody like me, but I thought maybe he'd accept my gift.

When I got to Simon's house, I was afraid to look at anybody or anything except Jesus. When I saw him across the room, I ran to him. Before I could change my mind, I threw myself at his feet, breaking the jar and releasing the heavy, sweet perfume and all the tears that had been bottled up for so long.

Simon and his guests were disgusted, but I kept pouring out all my poverty and pain at Jesus' feet. And he didn't stop me. Instead he let me wash his feet with my tears and dry them with my hair. And when I was done, he put his hand on my cheek and said, "Your sins are forgiven."[10] In front of all those people, he looked me in the eye and said, "You are more than your actions. You are a beloved child of God and you, too, can call him Father."

And now the man who freed me hangs in front of us, guarded by soldiers with swords and spears. A few of them gamble for Jesus' robe and belt. Somebody in the crowd yells, "Hey, Jesus, if you're really God, save yourself!" A criminal, hanging next to him, spits at Jesus.

Jesus watches them all. Then we hear him: "Father, forgive them, for they do not know what they are doing."[II]

(Looking above the audience at Jesus, incredulous) Forgive them? Forgive the people who worshiped you one day and turned on you the next? Forgive the people who beat you and nailed you to a cross? Forgive them?

(With mounting anger) Okay, so maybe I'm not one to judge. There are still plenty of people who hate me for what I was. But I knew what I was, and I came to you for forgiveness. You may have forgiven these people, but they either don't know it or don't care. One soldier makes an elaborate bow at the foot of this "king," soaking up the applause of the mob. In the crowd, eyes bulge and mouths water, feasting on the sights and smells of death. What difference has your forgiveness made to any of them?

(Still looking at Jesus) Painfully, Jesus raises his head and looks at me, gasping with the effort. But the pain in his eyes is more than physical. It's a pain that asks, "You still don't understand?"

(With dawning recognition) And then it hits me. Jesus offered me his forgiveness long before I ever came to him to ask for it. He offered me his forgiveness the very first moment he laid eyes on me. And what he did then was to help me to forgive myself.

(Struggles inwardly, then finally relents. As a prayer) Father, forgive them.

8

My Lord and My God

The Apostle Thomas

Scripture: John 20:24–28
Cast: 1 male
Props: None

MY PARENTS USED TO JOKE THAT MY FIRST WORDS WERE "PROVE IT." Apparently I was a sceptic right from the start. I needed hard evidence before I'd believe anything. It was pretty frustrating for my parents sometimes, not to mention my friends and my teachers. But, in my defence, even though I question things longer and louder than most people, once I've made up my mind I'll stand up for what I believe, even if it costs me.

So three years ago, when my friends told me somebody named Jesus from Nazareth was the Messiah, my response was, "Prove it." Some of them were excited, ready to drop everything and follow him. Not me. Not that fast. After all, plenty of other people had claimed to be the Messiah, but none of them could back it up.

The funny thing about Jesus, one of the things that set him apart from all those others, was that he never seemed set on proving he was the Messiah. In fact, sometimes he'd actually tell us *not* to tell people he was the Messiah.

In the end, it was his manner and miracles—especially his miracles—that convinced me. Tradition says that the

Messiah will be known by miracles that only he can perform, like healing someone from leprosy, healing someone who was blind from birth, and raising someone who'd been dead longer than three days. Jesus did all that and more. That sure got people's attention—not all of it positive. In fact, there were plenty of people who wanted to kill him for it.

But as Jesus' followers, we were ecstatic. The Messiah was here! And it was only a matter of time before he unleashed his power, got rid of the Romans, and set up his own kingdom.

What would it be like? Some of the guys and I would talk about it when Jesus was off praying. It's not that we were out for money or power. We really just wanted peace, prosperity, and justice for God's people. But we did like to picture ourselves helping run Jesus' kingdom, overseeing a new Israel that would grow and thrive under the Messiah's rule.

Two weeks ago, we thought it was all finally coming together. That Sunday, Jesus rode into Jerusalem with the crowds cheering, waving palm branches, and shouting, "Hosanna! Save us!" But it only took a few days for our dream to turn into a nightmare, with those same crowds yelling, "He's no king of ours! Crucify him!"

That Friday, I saw him hanging on a cross, his body limp. Our Messiah was dead. And we, his loyal followers, would-be officials in his kingdom, hung back on the fringes of the crowd, hoping nobody recognized us. Only hours before, we'd run away, abandoning Jesus. Some went into hiding, afraid they'd be next. But I couldn't. Not yet. I couldn't fathom that Jesus was dead. I refused to believe it until I'd seen it with my own eyes. Until I had proof.

The next day was the worst day of my life. We were all hiding in the upper room—all except Judas, who'd disappeared. We were scared, wondering whether the people who'd killed Jesus would be coming for us next. More than that, we were in shock, hardly able to believe that Jesus was gone.

The room echoed with memories of that other night—of Jesus washing our feet, praying over the cups of wine and breaking the bread, singing with us before we put on our cloaks and walked to Gethsemane.

But those were just echoes. There were a few murmurs in the room, but mostly we wrestled in silence with our questions, our shame. Peter took it the hardest. After all, three times he'd denied even knowing Jesus, just when Jesus needed him the most. But were the rest of us any better? We—I—ran away. We didn't even have the guts to follow Jesus to his trial like Peter did.

What happened to our dreams? To our king? How could things have gone so wrong? Was all my "proof" so worthless?

My mind kept running in circles—until the sound of the shofar interrupted my thoughts, the signal that the afternoon's sacrifice had been made. A lamb had been killed to take away our sins for another day. It reminded me of something, a memory—John, declaring in the wilderness, "Look, the Lamb of God, who takes away the sin of the world!"[12]

It seemed like an odd thing to say, and I'd pretty much dismissed it at the time. After all, John was a bit... eccentric. But now... well, some pretty odd things had been happening. People said that when Jesus died, the temple curtain, the one dividing the sanctuary from the Holy of Holies, tore in two. Right down the middle, top to bottom. They said it happened at the same time Jesus died, right when the shofar blew that afternoon.

Sacrifice. Lamb of God. Jesus.

Isaiah described the Messiah in terms of a sacrifice: "But he was pierced for our transgressions, he was crushed for our iniquities; the punishment that brought us peace was on him, and by his wounds we are healed."[13]

Could it be? Was it possible that Jesus hadn't come to be a king but a sacrifice? And if he did, what did that mean for us? For me?

The very next morning, a few people started saying Jesus was alive. We all went to the tomb, and it was just like Peter and Mary and the others had said. Empty. Grave clothes folded up neatly and no body to be seen. Most of them even saw him— Mary that morning in the garden, and the others in the upper room that night. Where was I? *(Chagrined)* Out buying food.

I knew I should believe them. They're my friends. We've been through thick and thin together these past few years, and I know I can trust them.

It was myself I had a hard time trusting. I'd wanted so badly, before, to believe that Jesus was something he wasn't. I mean, yes, he was the Messiah, but it wasn't anything like what we'd thought in the end.

What if that was the case again? I wanted so badly for him to be alive. Truly alive. I didn't doubt that the others had seen him. But what if it wasn't what they thought? What if he was just a spirit? A ghost?

They said he was living and breathing, as solid and real as any of us. And that he had the scars to prove it was really him—really crucified but alive again. Still, I wouldn't believe it, wouldn't let myself get my hopes up, until I proved it. Unless I saw the nail marks in his hands and put my finger where the nails had been, until I put my hand in his side, I wouldn't believe it. Couldn't believe it.

Not until I proved it.

But tonight, I know. It's true! Jesus really is alive. Not a ghost or spirit, but risen in the flesh!

I can't tell you what an agony the past week has been for me, wondering why Jesus appeared to everybody but me. Wondering whether maybe they'd been wrong after all. Or worse still, thinking maybe Jesus was angry at me because I was waiting for proof.

But tonight, we were all together again and suddenly Jesus was here with us. Even though the doors were locked, Jesus appeared out of nowhere, saying "Peace be with you!"[14]

And the very next thing he did, while I was still sitting there with my jaw on the floor, was hold out his hands to me. "Put your finger in my hands, Thomas," he said. "Put your hand in my side. Stop doubting and believe."[15]

There was no anger there, no guilt trip. Just an invitation. So I got up and did just what he said.

It hit me then like a flood—the thought that he truly was the Lamb of God, the sacrifice made once and for all for my doubt and my sin, all of it. And more than that. Jesus was the *risen* sacrifice, something completely unheard of and new. What did that mean?

Prophets sometimes raised the dead. Elijah did, and Elisha. Jesus, too, more than once. But who ever heard of the dead raising themselves? Who is this Jesus—not just a king with an earthly kingdom, but the sacrifice that takes away all our sin, and the one who in himself, alone, has power over death?

I looked into his eyes and knew that never again would I have to say "Prove it" to Jesus. Instead I fell at his feet and uttered the only words that were left to me: "My Lord and my God!"[16]

9

A Stranger at God's Table

Hannah

Scripture: 1 Samuel 1:1–28
Cast: 1 female
Props: A stool for Hannah to sit on
Small tunic, needle, and thread

(Hannah is sitting, sewing a small tunic, big enough for a five- or six-year-old. Throughout the monologue, the actor holds the tunic in such a way as to conceal her belly, until she stands at the end.)

IT'S FINISHED. JUST IN TIME, TOO. WE LEAVE FOR SHILOH tomorrow. Three times a year we celebrate festivals at the tabernacle there. You should see it—people coming by the thousands from all over Israel, the hillsides covered in tents, people dressed in their finest, the smells of all the sacrifices, the bleating of hundreds of sheep and goats and cattle... and the days and days of singing and dancing, feasting and special assemblies—it's enough to make your head spin.

For most of us, the festivals are the high points of our year. Not just because they're a break from work—although I'll admit, that's nice—but mainly because they're a chance to sit at God's table and fellowship with him. All the rest of the year, the priests at the tabernacle eat the sacred bread and the meat from the sacrifices on our behalf. But we Israelites are all consecrated to the Lord. At the festivals, we get to take our own places at God's table and enjoy his hospitality.

On top of that, the festivals are a chance to see family and friends from far away, to catch up on what's happened over the months—who's come of age, who's gotten married, who's had children...

(Trailing off, Hannah puts down the garment and looks off into the distance) You know, that's precisely why I used to hate going to Shiloh. When Elkanah and I were first married, going to the festivals was exciting—first as a new bride, and then picturing myself showing off a growing belly and then our newborn child. But festivals came and went. Other people's arms filled, but mine stayed empty. I started to dread the question: "So, Hannah, when will it be your turn?"

And then Elkanah married Peninnah. Oh, I never doubted he loved me. But he needed children, someone to pass along his inheritance to, and to look after him in his old age.

Even with Peninnah around, I knew Elkanah loved me. He went out of his way to show me that. And when I saw how other men treated their barren wives, like burdens or servants, I knew I should feel lucky. But that didn't make it any easier to see Peninnah have one child after another. Because that wasn't enough for her. She was jealous of the way Elkanah loved me and took every chance she got to flaunt her growing family. Especially at the festivals. Whenever the questions started, she was there, oozing false sympathy, saying "Poor Hannah," all the while gushing on and on about how God was blessing her.

She was even worse at the feast table. It killed her to see Elkanah give me a double helping of the food from our sacrifices. I knew it was just his way of telling me he loved me, even if I couldn't give him children. But that made things all the worse between Peninnah and me. When she passed me or sat next to me at the table, she'd hiss, "You hypocrite. How can you eat food sacrificed to God when you've obviously made him so angry that he's closed up your womb? You have no business being here."

Whether she knew it or not, Peninnah was just saying what I was already thinking. I mean, when God made his covenant with our people at Sinai, he promised us children as a sign of his blessing. So there must have been some reason he wasn't giving any to me. What was it? What had I done? I begged the Lord to show me, but all I got was silence.

And so, every year, I sat at those feasts, feeling more and more unwanted. Like a stranger at God's table. Especially at the Feast of Tabernacles. It was supposed to be a celebration of God's blessing us with fertile fields and abundant harvests. And there I was, with my barren womb—just a reminder that I wasn't part of that blessing—wondering whether God even wanted me at the table.

Finally, I couldn't take it anymore. We were at one of the Feasts of Tabernacles, and while everybody else ate and drank and exchanged news, I felt so sick and alone that I just got up from the table and ran. I could hear Elkanah calling, wondering where I was going, but I didn't even know myself. Was I running away from God, since he'd already turned his back on me? Or was I going to throw myself on his mercy one last time?

Without really thinking about it, I pushed my way through the crowds to the tabernacle, through the curtains into the courtyard. There was blood everywhere—on the altar, on the tables where they prepared the animals, on the ground. And in the middle of all that blood, I threw myself down and cried out to God, "What do you want from me? What more can I do? Tell me what I've done to cut myself off from your blessing and I'll do whatever it takes to make it right. O Lord Almighty, if you'll just turn your face to me—look at my misery and remember me—if you'll only give me a son, I'll give him back to you. I'll dedicate him to your service for the rest of his life. Just don't shut me out, Lord God. Please don't shut me out."

I guess I was creating quite a scene, rocking back and forth crying, covered in dust and blood, but I didn't care. I hardly even noticed, until I heard Eli. The old priest had been sitting by the entrance to the tabernacle, and when I looked up he was glaring at me, totally disgusted.

"Woman, you're a disgrace. How dare you come into a holy place slobbering drunk? Get out, and don't come back until you sober up!"

Just when I thought I'd hit bottom, there I was, being thrown out of the tabernacle by the High Priest himself. But I couldn't blame Eli. He looked so tired. It was his job to keep order in the tabernacle, to protect the holiness of the place. No small feat, especially during the chaos of the festivals.

So I said, "Please, sir, I haven't been drinking. I'm heart-broken and don't know what else to do except pour out my heart to God. So I've been praying here out of anguish and grief."

His face softened, and he said to me, "Go in peace, and may the God of Israel grant you what you have asked of him."[17]

Go in peace. I'd come to the sanctuary pleading with God for a child, and in his grace he answered the deeper cry of my heart. Because it wasn't just Eli speaking. As high priest, Eli's our intercessor—our representative before God, and God's spokesman to us. Through Eli, God offered me shalom, his peace. In that one word, he told me that I was complete in him, that he gave me his blessing, too. Oh, I didn't know at the time whether I'd ever have the child I longed for, but I knew that I was welcome at God's table.

And that's where I went—right back to the table. It didn't matter that Peninnah was there or what anybody said. It just felt good to take my place and drink in God's blessing, however he chose to pour it out on me.

(Stands up, shakes out the garment in front of her and folds it.) And now I have another reason to look forward to our trips to Shiloh. My son Samuel is there, serving God in the sanctuary just like I'd promised. God's been good to Elkanah and me; he's blessed us richly. It's like the song I sang when we dedicated Samuel at the tabernacle: "The Lord raises the poor from the dust and lifts the needy from the ash heap; he seats them with princes and has them inherit a throne of honour."[18]

For me, that throne of honour is the seat God offers me at his banquet, because whatever happens I know I'm not a stranger at God's table. I am welcome there.

(Turns to exit. As she turns, she places her hand on her belly so the audience can see that she is pregnant.)

10

Trusting God in Uncertain Times

Jochebed

Scripture: Exodus 1:1—2:10
Cast: 1 female
Props: Doll wrapped in blanket
Basket
Table

(Jochebed enters, carrying a baby and singing a lullaby to soothe him. There is a table centre stage with a large basket on it. She places the baby in the basket)

HE'S ASLEEP. *(LOOKING NERVOUSLY OUT WINDOW)* MIRIAM'S GONE ON ahead, and we'll soon have to go, too.

Amram and I have been talking this over for days. It's the only way to save our son. Now that it's time, though, I don't know if I can go through with it...

But what choice do we have? The Egyptians are slaughtering our baby boys. I don't understand why they hate us so much. For generations, our people have lived here in Goshen, at peace with the Egyptians. Suddenly, Pharaoh thinks we're a threat? That we're going to rise up against him? We have no quarrel with him or his people. And we've given them no reason to have any issues with us. Quite the opposite, actually. Wasn't it Joseph, one of us, who saved their skins during the great famine?

And why would we want to take over Egypt? God promised us a land of our own, in Canaan. Oh, I know some of our people are getting too settled in Goshen. They're starting to follow the Egyptians' ways and worship their gods. But isn't that all the more reason for us to leave Egypt?

Not like any of that matters to Pharaoh. Just last week, the soldiers came and took Levi and Hannah's little boy and threw him in the river. They made Levi and Hannah watch while the Nile swallowed him up. Poor Hannah—she hasn't eaten or talked to anybody ever since little Avram... (*Shudders*)

Any time now, they'll come for our son, too. Amram and I have prayed desperately for a miracle to save our baby. But what about Hannah and Levi? What about all those other parents whose miracles never came?

And yet it seems ours just might. I sent Miriam down to the riverbank a few days ago to pick papyrus reeds to make baskets, and that's where she saw Pharaoh's daughter, Neferatu, coming down with her attendants to bathe. Miriam was terrified of what the princess would do if she found her, a Hebrew, lurking in the reeds while she was bathing. So she hid, waiting for the princess to leave.

But the princess didn't leave. Instead, after she bathed the princess put baskets of flowers and food and incense on the water, and began praying to Khnum... you know, one of the Egyptians' river gods. They say Khnum creates their children out of the silt of the Nile. We'd heard the princess was childless, and here she was praying to Khnum for a child of her own.

Maybe, just maybe, this will be Yahweh's answer to our prayers. We know that the Egyptians adopt children when they can't have any of their own. If the princess finds a child there by the river's edge, maybe she'll think Khnum has answered her prayers.

I know what you're thinking. How can we give up our child, a child of the Promise, to live as an Egyptian, not knowing God? But what choice do we have? Besides, Shiphrah and Puah, our midwives, often talk about how well the Egyptians treat their children's nurses, almost as if they're the children's own mothers. If the princess takes our baby to be her son, she'll need somebody to nurse him. Somebody like me.

So I've been sending Miriam back to the river every day to watch and see when the princess comes down to bathe, so we'll know when we can expect her to be there. I've taken the reeds Miriam collected and woven a basket for my son. I've coated it with tar and pitch to make it waterproof. And I've grilled Miriam on the speech that she's to make when the princess finds our baby in the basket: "Your Highness, the Hebrew women are strong and bear many children. Do you want me to bring one who can nurse this baby for you?"

I've done all I can—made my plans, woven the basket, prepared Miriam, and fed my baby so he won't wake up when I carry him down to the river. All I have left is to put the basket in the river. If only I could control what happens after that. With every fibre of my being, I just want to hold on to my child. But the only way to save him is to let him go. Yahweh, give me the strength to place my child—our future—into your hands.

(Covers her head with scarf and, taking long look at the baby, picks up basket and exits.)

11

Is He the One?

John the Baptist

Scripture: Matthew 11:1–6
Cast: 1 male
Props: None

(John is dressed in ragged clothes, his hair and beard dishevelled.)

WHEN YOU'RE LOCKED IN A DUNGEON, THE MOST TORMENTING thought, the one your mind keeps circling back to, is what you miss most about freedom. About life aboveground.

Most of the men here miss the sun more than anything. Maybe not at first. At first they miss their families and friends. They miss being able to walk where they choose, having enough to eat or a blanket to sleep under. But sooner or later, when everyone's forgotten about them, when all hope of freedom is gone, most of them simply miss the sun.

I can understand that. The darkness here is unnatural; it swallows up night and day, all sense of time and existence. It's the shadow of death, of being utterly abandoned by man and by God.

But what I miss most of all is the wind.

When I lived in the wilderness, the sun was impersonal. Its searing light and scorching heat were the indifferent messengers of a distant master. But there was nothing indifferent about the wind. It sought me out, probing with its long thin fingers into every crack and crevice of the rocks. It prodded and challenged, daring me to try to stand against it.

The sun was predictable. I knew the paths it would take. But the wind would rear up without warning, change its course on a whim. It made me feel alive. Like the cliffs around me, I was hewed and honed by the wind, all pride and pretence chiselled away until all that was left was raw and real. Some days I'd climb the cliffs and hurl my voice into the wind, just to feel my passion flowing into God's own, swept along by the torrent of judgment soon to be unleashed. The wind was a force to be grappled with like the angel who visited Jacob—battering me, daring me to wrestle with it and not run away. Just like I wrestled with God.

Now our leaders in Israel want a God like the sun, one they can enjoy when they want and find shade from when they've had enough. They hide from him behind their laws and their pride, their status as sons of Abraham. But the storm is coming, the wind that will strip away their pretence until God confronts them face to face.

"Repent!" I cried out to them. "Get rid of your pride and false security. Engage with God, now, in righteousness and repentance. You were once the threshing sledge of the Lord, the instrument of his judgment on his enemies. God declared, 'You will winnow them, the wind will pick them up, and a gale will blow them away.'[19] But now, beware! You are the grain the Lord is about to thresh." I called out, "His winnowing fork is in his hand, and he will clear his threshing floor, gathering his wheat into the barn and burning up the chaff with unquenchable fire."[20]

I was so sure that Jesus would be the one God sent to purify Israel and establish his kingdom. Israel, at least a remnant, would turn back to the Lord, and he'd deliver us from bondage. Israel would be great again, with the Chosen One, the Son of David, sitting in power on an everlasting throne.

But now, I don't know. The question tortures me: Is Jesus the one who was to come, or should we expect someone else?

It used to seem so clear. So clear. When Jesus came to the river to be baptized, the heavens opened and God's own voice declared Jesus his Son. I thought the time had come. How fitting that the carpenter from Nazareth, a man used to wielding saw and axe, would be wielding God's instruments of judgment. "Repent!" I called out. "Produce fruit in keeping with repentance.[21] The ax is already at the root of the trees, and every tree that does not produce good fruit will be cut down and thrown into the fire."[22] Surely the day of the Lord was near.

I still believed it when I was arrested and thrown into this dungeon for speaking out against King Herod. What a perfect opportunity for Jesus to act, to openly denounce the corruption of Israel's rulers and unleash God's judgment.

And so we waited, my disciples and I, for the day of the Lord. But that day still hasn't come. Jesus still just travels around, preaching repentance. I'm told he forbids his disciples to talk about the healings he's performed, or to tell anyone he's the Messiah. We keep waiting for him to march in and claim his rightful throne. So why doesn't he act? Is he the one, or should we wait for someone else? I keep asking God, but he doesn't answer.

That's what torments me most of all in this dungeon: God's silence. I'm not afraid for my life. I'm ready to die, if it will help establish the Messiah's kingdom. But I don't understand why God is suddenly silent. I don't doubt God called me—it was prophesied by an angel even before I was conceived. But maybe I've been wrong about Jesus. Maybe he's just another prophet, sent like me to help prepare the way for the promised one. If only God would speak to me. I'm not afraid of his rebuke, just his silence.

(Crying out) Speak to me, God—even if you tell me I was wrong about Jesus. Just talk to me! Wrestle with me again! All my life, you've been my passion. So use me. Use me up. Drain me to the dregs, but don't abandon me. *(Anguished)* Please just tell me. Is Jesus the one?

(His emotion spent) Here in this windless dungeon, the air is lifeless. Its chill seeps into my skin and bones like decay. I long to feel the wind moving, to stand in the storm, seeing the mighty and unrighteous brought down. Yet what was it they told me? That Jesus himself calmed a storm. They say he and his disciples were crossing the sea in a boat, and a storm arose, that in order to save his terrified disciples Jesus calmed the wind itself. With just a word.

Can it be true? Is Jesus the One? I long to feel the wind. And yet they say that Jesus commands the wind. I want to see him wield the winnowing fork of God's judgment. Yet Jesus also described Israel as a field full of wheat and weeds; he said that it wasn't time yet to pull up the weeds, or the young stalks of wheat would be pulled up, too. Jesus calmed the storm for the sake of some frightened men. Is it possible that he's also withholding his hand until the weak—the poor, the blind and deaf and lame on whom he lavishes his time—have been strengthened? So that they can withstand the wind and the winnow when they come? I don't know. I just don't know.

Lord God, I know my time here is short. All I ask from you, before you're done with me, is one word, one breath. That's all. Should we expect someone else? Or is Jesus the One?

12

Running from God

Gomer

Scripture: Hosea 1:1-10, 3:1-5
Cast: 1 female
Props: None

(Gomer enters and addresses the audience. There is something of the rebel about her, a defiance that hides a deeper vulnerability.)

SOMETIMES YOUR JOURNEY WITH GOD BEGINS WHILE YOU THINK you're running away from him.

Walking with God never used to be a big deal to me. I mean, first of all, which god? People here in Judah worship lots of different gods. Yahweh's just one. There's also Baal, Asherah, Ashtoreth, Molech, Chemosh... Some people worship all of them. You know, make sure they've covered all the angles. Other people pick and choose, depending on what they want at the time. For lots of people, Yahweh's got way too many rules. If you're looking for a good time, gods and goddesses like Baal and Asherah—they're the way to go. And I was definitely looking for a good time.

See, I was never one of the "good girls." You know the type—always cooking and cleaning and sewing. Keeping their eyes down and their voices quiet, and never talking to strange men. Me, I was always getting into trouble for being *(mimicking)* "too loud," "too bold," "too high-spirited." Try "too mind-numbingly bored." It was just a matter of time before my parents got me out of their faces by marrying me off to some farmer or shepherd—the further out in the country, the better. Like I was going to stick around waiting for that to happen.

I'd heard they were always looking for girls to work at Asherah's shrine. I knew if I showed up there, I'd get a place to stay, beautiful clothes, and something more exciting than cleaning the muck off some farmer's feet or raising my own flock of little shepherds.

So I took off. My parents went ballistic, but seriously, what was the big deal? I mean, they worshiped at the shrine, too. But I guess having their daughter working there was a bit much, even for them. They figured the only way to get some respectability back was to marry me off. Not that finding somebody who'd take damaged goods would be easy. But one day they showed up at the shrine, grabbed me, and forced me to come back home with them, telling me they'd arranged for me to get married to, get this, *(scornfully)* Hosea.

Do you have any idea what it's like to be married to a prophet? To live your entire life as somebody's sermon illustration? Especially after what I'd just come from. Come on! I couldn't walk down the street without some busybody saying, "What on earth possessed Hosea to marry her?"

Yeah, well, I didn't ask to be anybody's object lesson. You know, I actually tried to be the "good wife" for a while. I cooked Hosea's meals and cleaned his house. I even gave him a son. But we had nothing in common. What were we supposed to talk about over dinner? *(Sickly sweet)* "How was your day, dear?" *(Mimicking Hosea's voice)* "Oy, you should know for days. I spent the whole afternoon on the corner of Temple Avenue and Market Street, yelling at the crowds. Boy, is my throat ever sore." *(Rolls eyes)*

So I started going back to the shrine. At first, I snuck out whenever Hosea left the house, but pretty soon I didn't bother trying to hide where I was going. There was no point. Anybody with two eyes could see that my next two children looked nothing like Hosea.

Still, he insisted on naming them. Or, more to the point, he said that God had named them. Check this out: "Lo-Ruhamah" and "Lo-Ammi." "Not Loved" and "Not My People." Talk about giving the kids a complex.

To be honest, though, I was the one standing between my children and Hosea. I knew I could use them to hurt him, because I could see in his eyes that he loved them and wanted to be a father to them just as much as he was to his own son. God only knows why.

And then Shallum came to the shrine. By this time, there were plenty of girls at the temple who were younger and... "fresher" than I was, but I was the one Shallum kept coming back to. Being with a rich wine merchant was certainly more interesting than being the wife of some crazy prophet. So when Shallum asked me to leave the shrine and come live with him, I dropped Hosea and the kids like hot coals. It didn't take long, though, to realize that Shallum wasn't looking for a "life partner." Turns out he was in debt up to his eyeballs and saw me as a... marketable commodity, if you know what I mean. And when that didn't bring in enough to pay his creditors, they sold us both off as slaves.

You're probably thinking I had that coming. Yeah, well, maybe I did. But I figured that after all I'd done to serve Asherah, the least she could do was get me out of this mess. So I prayed to her and burned incense. I begged and I pleaded, but... nothing. If she was there at all, she either didn't hear or didn't care.

In the end, the one who rescued me, even though he didn't owe me any favours, was Yahweh.

The day Hosea walked into my master's house, I thought maybe he'd come to gloat. But when he pulled out a bag of silver and said he'd come to buy me back, I realized he probably had an even sweeter revenge in mind. He was going to make me his own slave—humiliate me in front of my own children and all those nosy neighbours.

But when we got to Hosea's house, instead of putting me to work, he put me in this room and barred the door. He told me, "You're living with me now, and you're not going to see any other men. Your days as a prostitute are over."

Great. First a slave, now a prisoner. *(Sarcastic)* Big improvement. Except that Hosea was the strangest jailer I'd ever heard of. The first morning, Hosea brought me bread that he'd baked himself. He washed my feet and brought me a new robe to wear. And every evening, he'd bring me dinner and serve me himself. Then he'd recite to me—psalms, poetry, King Solomon's love song.

I couldn't figure it out. I mean, the men I'd tried to please treated me like trash, while the man I'd treated like trash treated me like a princess. Don't get me wrong. Hosea wasn't grovelling and snivelling at my feet. There was just a quietness to him, a persistence and strength I hadn't stopped to notice before.

At first I tried to push him away—I insulted his cooking, told him he was pathetic. But he seemed to see right through me, and pretty soon I felt ashamed. So I started asking him about himself, learning things I'd never bothered to find out before. And I started telling him some of my darker secrets, testing him to see when he'd push me away. But the more I shared with him, the more I hoped he'd let me stay. And one day I realized the door wasn't barred anymore—and hadn't been for a long time. Because Hosea had never intended to imprison me, but to draw me into relationship.

That's what Hosea's been trying to tell us all along. While we're busy running away from God, God is pursuing us. Not like a hunter or a slave master, but like a father or a true lover, the way Hosea pursued me.

I hate to think where I'd have ended up if Hosea hadn't pursued me. But he did, and his pursuit led me here—to a place I thought was a prison but that turned out to be the place where relationship could happen. A relationship with someone who'd seen the very worst of me and chose to love me anyway.

Obedience to God is like this house and his rules are like the walls. They don't imprison us. Instead they mark out the boundaries, the place where relationship with God can happen—relationship with the one who knows us most deeply and loves us most passionately. Relationship with the only one who can free us from everything that enslaves us.

I thank God that even when I was running away from him, he was right there with me. Pursuing me. Calling me back into relationship with him. *(Looks up as if she hears a voice offstage, and smiles)*

And now, if you'll excuse me, I'd like to get going. Hosea will be home soon and I'm looking forward to having dinner with him. We've got a lot to talk about. *(Exits)*

13

Out of the Shadows

Mary Magdalene

Scripture: Luke 8:2, Romans 8:1-2
Cast: 1 female
Props: Large water jar

(Mary enters carrying a large jar on her shoulder and sets it down centre stage.)

I SAW HER AT THE WELL TODAY. SHE WAS HIDING IN THE SHADOWS between the houses. And she looked thirsty. Not for water. She can get that easily enough when the sun's high and the other women have left to sit where it's cool, to spin or weave and gossip.

She was thirsty for acceptance, to be included in their circle, sharing news and laughter. But she knows that if she ever tries to join them, the other women will grab their water jars, gather their skirts around them, and scatter.

I know, because I used to be just like her.

Crazy Mary, they called me back in Magdala—among other things I'd rather not repeat.

It wasn't always that way. When I was little, I was my mother's pet. I had lots of friends. There was nothing unusual about me, except maybe a restlessness, an imagination that had me daydreaming when I should have been getting my work done. But nothing that even hinted at what was coming.

Then, around the time I became a woman, the voices and visions started. At first they were just flashes, sights or sounds that made me stop what I was doing and look around to see who was there. They were easy enough to explain away—the wind blowing a curtain, children shouting in the distance. But soon they became stranger, sinister. They whispered of dangers all around me, told me to do unspeakable things. I'd always been afraid of snakes, but now I saw them everywhere—crawling under doors, slithering around my feet and up my arms—until I grabbed a knife to cut them off me. I remember one night seeing scorpions swarming over my mother while she slept. I took a torch and waved it over her to scare them off until she woke up screaming in terror—of me.

Suddenly, my friends avoided me. My parents were ashamed of me. When the voices and visions were at their worst, my parents would lock me in a room by myself, afraid of what I'd do to myself or them. At other times, when the voices were quieter, they'd let me out but watch me like hawks. A few times, my mother tried to take me with her to the well, but the other women would shy away from us. Their children would throw stones.

Pretty soon I stopped going, and secretly, I think, my mother was relieved. Most of the time I stayed home, afraid to go out. I didn't want to be seen that way, and I was afraid of what the voices would make me do next. I was scared and suspicious all the time. I couldn't even trust my own senses, because I didn't know what was real and what was demonic.

Some days, though, when I was thinking more clearly, I'd be overwhelmed with loneliness. I knew I could never have friends again, never live a normal life, sharing daily chores with other women. But I wanted to pretend I was still one of them. So I'd sneak out of the house and make my way through the shadows to the well. There was a low wall I could hide behind, close enough to listen to their gossip. I'd smile to myself, pretending they were telling me their stories and secrets. I'd imagine what I'd say, and whisper my answers to the wind.

I really must have looked crazy, rocking and whispering to myself, lost in my own world. No wonder people called me Crazy Mary, even on my better days. And little did they know the torture I went through on my bad days, locked away, screaming in pain, clawing at my hair and skin to try and drive the demons away.

But nobody could drive them away. Every time my parents heard of some new rabbi who could drive out demons, they'd take me to see him. Each time, as soon as the chanting and prayers started, the demons would take a tighter hold of me, until the rabbis would give up and send us away. It was as if the demons were flaunting their power over anybody who tried to tear me from their claws.

And then the rabbi from Nazareth came. I thought, *Yeah, sure, what could he possibly do that the others haven't already tried?* But then we heard people talking about other miracles he'd performed—turning water into wine, making a paralyzed man walk. They said he could heal the blind and the leper with just a touch. Even people like me.

So they took me to see him—my parents and several friends they'd recruited to drag me to where Jesus was. And the demons fought back again. But this time, they seemed different. This time, it was like they were afraid. As if they knew Jesus was somebody they couldn't scare away.

My parents tell me that when Jesus walked through the crowd toward us, I was like a wild animal, screaming and rolling around on the ground, my face and arms streaked with their blood and my own. That when he reached toward me, I cowered and whimpered, snarling but unable to lash out.

All *I* remember is that when Jesus spoke, everything went quiet. That when he said, "You evil spirits, I command you to come out of her and never enter her again," there was one final convulsion and then... peace. As if all the space inside me that had been filled with filth and fear was suddenly clean and filled with light. As if I could suddenly see through my own eyes again. And I fell at the feet of the one who had healed me and worshiped him, because he alone had God's own power to set me free.

I've been following Jesus ever since. I mean, how could I not want to be where he is? To be filled every day with his light and truth? To see him reach out to heal people who are as sick and broken as I was?

To be honest, at first I followed Jesus not just out of love, but fear, too. Because every so often I'd hear echoes of those voices that used to torment me, and I'd be afraid they were coming back, taking control of me again. I was afraid to let Jesus out of my sight, because I didn't want to go back to what I'd been.

But Jesus taught me that those echoes aren't the demons; they're just the memory of them. And those memories don't have the power to possess me, or to condemn me. Not in Jesus' sight, or in God's.

Sometimes it's still tempting to condemn myself when I remember what I was, or when I meet other people who still see me that way. But the more I'm with Jesus, the more I learn to see myself the way he sees me. Now, one look at Jesus is usually all it takes to remind me that I'm free. His other followers, too—the ones who really know him—pour on me the acceptance for which I used to thirst. After all, they know that, one way or another, we've all been set free.

What about you? How has Jesus' touch set you free? Do voices from the past still come back to condemn you for what you've been or done? Those voices are just echoes, memories. They don't have the power to condemn what Jesus has pronounced clean.

When I hear those voices, I try to let them remind me of all Jesus has done for me, and all that I have to be thankful for. And the best way I know of to thank Jesus is to show others the acceptance that Jesus offers. And so, today, I took my water jar and walked over to the woman in the shadows. I sat beside her—they tell me her name's Abigail—and we shared a cup of water. She didn't say much; I think she was afraid to. But when I touched her hand to say goodbye, I think I saw the beginning of a smile.

I'll be looking for her at the well tomorrow. I hope she's there. And, you know, something tells me she will be.

14

I Don't Understand You

Sarah

Scripture: Genesis 22:1–14
Cast: 1 female
Props: A small stool or bench
A piece of fabric, needle, and thread

(Sarah is sitting alone in her tent, sewing. She's an elderly woman and moves somewhat slowly and uncomfortably. She looks up suddenly, rises, walks forward, and mimes peering out the entrance to her tent.)

(CALLING) IS THAT YOU, ABRAHAM? *(EXASPERATED)* WHERE ON earth did you go this time? Aren't you coming in to say hello?

(Seeing Isaac, and stepping aside as he enters tent) Isaac, welcome home! That was a long trip. *(Jokingly)* I was beginning to wonder if I'd ever see you again.

(Walking back to seat, waving off help) No, no, I'm fine. I'm just not a young woman anymore. Not like I was when you were born.... That was a joke, son.

(Sits down, peering at doorway) Where is your father? What do you mean, watering the donkey? He usually gets one of the servants to do that. *(Shrugs)* Well, never mind. So tell me, where did you and your father go to make sacrifices this time?... Moriah? That's further than usual. Your father must have had something very important to pray about. Did you meet anyone along the way? Hear any news?

You're very quiet. Oh, listen to me! You've had a long journey and here I am, prattling on. Let me get one of the servants to draw you some water and wash your feet... Later? All right.

(Looking expectantly at Isaac, and eventually breaking the silence, just to make conversation) I heard you and your father left without taking any animals along for the sacrifice. I know Abraham was in a hurry, but he doesn't usually forget things like that. What did you use for a sacrifice? *(Starts, then recovers)* Isaac, you know better than to tease me like that... *(With dawning realization)* You're not teasing.

(Face darkening, she starts to rise, then sits again as though Isaac is guiding her back down) Don't tell me to calm down. You tell me *exactly* what your father did on that mountain. *(Listens, then repeats)* He built an altar, tied you up on it, and was about to slit your throat... *(Sarcastically)* Oh, *God* provided a ram to take your place. *(Exploding)* I don't care if God provided a *thousand* rams to take your place on that altar. What was Abraham thinking? *(Darkly)* God told him to do it?

(Getting up) Out of my way! *(Walks to tent entrance and yells)* Abraham! Abraham!! You show your face this instant. *(Signalling someone walking by)* Where is Abraham? *(Turns back into tent, incredulous)* He left the camp. I should have known. He just tried to sacrifice my only son to his God. Of course he's not going to show his face in here. *(To Isaac)* No, instead he sends you to break the news to me... Overreacting? I haven't even *begun* to react! What—you're leaving, too? Fine. Go hide with your father until I've finished "overreacting"!

(Pacing angrily) Sacrifice. *(Stops and looks up)* You want a sacrifice? I'll give you a sacrifice. How about a 120-year-old man, huh? *(Pacing again, sarcastic)* God told him to do it. To kill the son I waited ninety years to have.

(Looking up) Why? Why me? Why would you do this to me? Sacrifice! Haven't I given up enough for you? We had everything. When we lived in Ur, we were rich. We were influential. We had all the comforts of a civilized life. Then, out of the blue, you speak to Abraham—you, a God nobody else had ever heard of—and you tell him to leave it all behind. Did I argue? Well, okay, I did. But I went along with it in the end. For years, I've wandered with Abraham and this... rabble through the wilderness. I've lived among these uncouth Canaanites. And I've held my tongue!

Yes, I know you've blessed us. We're rich. We have flocks and herds like I've never seen before. But we have no home! You keep promising Abraham a land, something permanent, a legacy we can pass down to our children and our children's children. And yet we're still wandering.

And children! Lord God, Almighty, I know you've blessed us with a son. He's all I could ever have hoped for and more. But do you have any *idea* of the agony I went through, waiting? To see my youth come and go, with no sign of a child? To feel my hope bleeding away with every stillbirth and miscarriage, until I was too old to hope anymore?

And then you came, and you promised Abraham descendants as numerous as the dust of the earth or the stars in the sky. It felt like you were mocking me. Old, barren Sarai. God has this wonderful plan that he'll be carrying out right under your nose and you don't get to be a part of it.

I don't understand you. At least with the gods we worshipped in Ur, I knew what to do. When they seemed angry, I knew how to appease them. When I wanted something, I knew what sacrifices to make. Those gods spoke through their priests and priestesses. *You* I can't figure out. You appear to Abraham, that I can understand. He's a wealthy man, the head of an important household. I'm a woman. I didn't expect you to

56

come to me. *(Contemptuously)* But then Hagar, my slave, comes back from the wilderness talking about how you sent an angel to her. What about *me*? You seem to appear to everybody else. But the only way I get to hear from you—I, the mistress of this entire household—is by hiding behind a tent flap and eavesdropping on you.

(Imploring) I don't understand you. What was I supposed to do? You didn't seem to be doing anything, so I took matters into my own hands. I gave Hagar to Abraham, to see if he could father a child with her. And I've had nothing but grief from that woman and her brat ever since. Are you satisfied?

Then, finally, after years of only promises, you gave us Isaac. Wasn't I duly grateful? At the age of ninety, I gave birth and nursed a child. Who was I to deny how miraculous that was?

Yes, your promise came true, and I gave you all the credit. What more do you want from me? Tell me, and I'll do it. You've given us everything—flocks, herds, servants, riches. I showed you once, when we left Ur, that I was willing to give up everything. I'll do it again if you ask me to. But not Isaac. After all we've been through, how could you ask me to give up Isaac?

Abraham has his riches, and some day he'll have this land. He'll have his legacy; he'll be remembered. But without Isaac, what do *I* have? All I have, the only lasting mark I can leave on this earth, is my son. How can you taunt me by threatening to take him away?

You are the God of all the earth. *Everything* is yours—the earth, the heavens, everything in them. One life, more or less, probably doesn't make any difference to you. It's different for me. Isaac is all I have and, in the end, all I *am*. But then how could you, the God of the universe, possibly know what it's like to lose your only son?

I don't understand you.

15

Vision Revision

Saul

Scripture: Acts 9:1–19
Cast: 1 male
Props: Table and stool

(One stool stands centre stage, with a table upstage and off to side. Saul enters from side of stage. Newly blind, he gropes slowly around the table and toward the stool, carefully climbs on, and sits. He faces audience, but looks above or past them as he speaks, eyes unfocused. During monologue, Saul can get up and move around, but always groping his way.)

THERE. AT LEAST IT'S STILL WHERE I REMEMBER IT. *(ANGRILY)* Yesterday I was traveling from Jerusalem to Damascus, making my own way over hills and through wilderness. Today I can barely find my way across this room without cracking my shins on the table or breaking my nose on the doorframe.

But I refuse to be led around by the hand like a child. Not in here, at least. Here, in this room, I'm still a man. Out there, I'm not sure what I am anymore.

Yesterday, it was all perfectly clear. I was Saul, a Pharisee. I was doing God's work, cleansing Israel from The Way. Today I'm in the dark. Literally and figuratively.

At the Crossroads

What do you do when everything you know, everything on which you've built your life, is pulled out from under you? Until yesterday, my life was devoted to the Law. From childhood on, I studied it: first in Tarsus, and then in Jerusalem under Rabbi Gamaliel, the most respected rabbi in Israel.

The Law, the distillation of God's will and nature, is what sets Israel apart from every other nation. It's the door through which we enter into relationship with the Holy One. And as a Pharisee, by studying and following all the minutiae of the Law, I'm part of a revolution of holiness that will reveal the Almighty's kingdom in Israel in all its fullness.

At least, I was.

When this Jesus began traveling around, making preposterous claims that he was the Son of God, that he had authority to forgive sins and judge our traditions, I helped collect the evidence against him, until he was arrested and crucified for his blasphemy. And then, when his followers began spreading the rumour that he'd risen from the dead, and teaching that Jesus—not the Law—was the way to salvation, I devoted myself to finding them and wiping them out.

We'd already caught quite a few of these followers of The Way around Jerusalem. Those who didn't recant their beliefs and turn back to God's Law were killed—as they deserved. And now I have written permission from the High Priest himself to search synagogues in Damascus and bring back any followers of The Way that we find here to stand trial in Jerusalem.

I was convinced we were doing God's will. After all, the prophets denounced impurity. The history of Israel shows that blasphemers and idolaters have to be destroyed. It's what God wants!

Isn't it?

It's frightening how quickly everything you think you know can be taken away.

After nearly five days on the road, we were just a few hours away from Damascus. We were planning what we'd do when we arrived at the synagogue when a blinding flash of light stopped us dead in our tracks. I fell to the ground, shielding my eyes with my arm. And out of the light, a voice called, "Saul, Saul, why do you persecute me?"[23]

Persecute God? No! I was *serving* him.

So I asked, "Who are you, Lord?"[24]

And the voice answered, "I am Jesus, whom you are persecuting."[25]

Jesus? The one we crucified? The one whose resurrection was only a rumour? It couldn't be. Yet all my companions saw the flash of light and heard the voice, too. And when I took my arm away from my eyes, I was blind.

Do you have any idea how it feels to be led around by the hand like a child, helpless, uncertain? I can't find my way down the road, or even to a table or bed by myself. I can only grope my way around this room, and the slightest change in the position of a table or chair will send me sprawling.

But even worse than the physical blindness is the spiritual blindness. The feeling that the God to whom I've devoted my whole life is suddenly a stranger. Where's the justice in that? I've spent my life studying God's Law so I can follow it perfectly. Jesus openly broke the Law, healing and allowing his followers to pick grain on the Sabbath. I keep myself ritually clean. Jesus ate with tax collectors; he touched unclean women and lepers. I worship God in the temple that God himself commanded us to build. Jesus bragged that he'd tear the temple down.

Jesus was a blasphemer, directly assaulting God's holy Law that I've worked all my life to uphold. And yet *I'm* struck blind. Blind, like the men of Sodom in their sin or the army of Aram who attacked Elisha. Why? Am I no better than the Sodomites? Am I God's enemy rather than his servant?

What am I supposed to think? That everything to which I've devoted my life is false? That the God I thought I knew is a stranger? Everything I know, everything I am, tells me that God's Law is true, that his commands are real and binding. Yet the power that stopped me dead in my tracks and struck me blind is real, too. How am I supposed to reconcile the two?

I've learned, in a short time, to grope my way around this room. I know I can learn to live with physical blindness, if that's what God intends for me. But how do I learn to live without my spiritual sight?

After a lifetime of seeing God one way, finding out that I saw him all wrong is terrifying. Part of me just wants to go back to what was, to the familiar, rather than learning to serve a God who's a stranger. But to go back now would be a blindness of my own choosing.

If God has struck me with not only a physical blindness but a spiritual one, he must have a reason. Maybe in taking away *my* vision he's trying to open my eyes to *his*. I don't know whether or not God will ever choose to restore my physical sight. But I can choose to invite him to restore my spiritual sight.

(Raising hands and turning face upwards) Lord God, Lord Jesus, as hard as it is for me to be led by the hand, I reach out to you now. Guide me through the unknown and help me learn to know you. Whatever new sight I gain, physically or spiritually, I want it to come from you. Because it's better to have a physical blindness that comes from you than a spiritual blindness of my own choosing.

16

As for Me and My Household

Joshua

Scripture: Joshua 24:1–15
Cast: 1 male
Props: None

(An elderly Joshua enters, walks to front of stage, and holds out arms to audience in welcome.)

WELCOME, MY FRIENDS. WELCOME. I AM JOSHUA, SON OF NUN. I'm so glad you've come to celebrate the Passover with my family and me. Come in, come in. We'll be starting soon.

I'm told some of you have never celebrated the Passover before. Well, let me explain a bit about it. Tonight we'll feast and remember the night of the firstborn, a night of consecration. We'll tell the story and share the bread and herbs, the charoset and lamb. We'll sit back and enjoy each other's company.

So please, join us. Sit down and relax. You're among friends. Not that we could sit down and relax that night. *That* night... well, let me tell you about that night.

That night, nobody sat. A few days earlier, after months of waiting while Pharaoh kept changing his mind, Moses had told us it was finally time to get ready to leave Egypt. He told us to prepare a special meal to eat while we waited to go. So we stood around the table with our traveling cloaks on, our sandals on our feet, and our staffs in our hands. Everything we owned—well, everything we could carry—was packed and waiting by the door.

Everybody was alert as we passed around the bread—not the usual soft bread, but flat crisp bread made without yeast, made in a hurry because we didn't know when we'd get the signal to go.

And as we stood, we ate the lamb. Four days earlier, I'd chosen a young male lamb from our flock. A perfect lamb. The best we had. Then, on the night of the feast, my oldest son Ephraim and I killed it. I took a branch, dipped it in the lamb's blood, and spread the blood on the doorframe of our house. All around us, our neighbours were doing the same thing. Then we called our families together. I watched my children as they walked through the doorway and wondered whether the blood would be enough to keep my eldest, Ephraim, safe from what Moses had said would happen. Whether I could trust it to keep me safe, because I'm a firstborn, too.

It wasn't easy learning to trust our ancestors' God. We'd been in Egypt for four hundred years. Sure, our parents had told us the stories of Abraham and Isaac, Jacob and Joseph—of their travels from Ur to Canaan and Egypt, and the promise that their God would one day make us a nation and give us a land of our own. But our people worshiped the Egyptian gods, too. Those of you who only worship one God might judge us for that, but you have to understand, that was all we knew. The nations around us all served many gods, and it was no big deal to them to add one more to the mix. Why should it have been any different for us? Our God might have been there to help Joseph read Pharaoh's dreams a long time ago, but when the pharaohs turned against us and made us their slaves our God seemed to get pretty quiet. So we adapted. We held on to our hope that someday God would make good on his promise, but in the meantime we kept our options open and prayed to the Egyptian gods, too.

Then along came Moses and Aaron, claiming God had said it was time to set us free. Of course, we wanted proof that God had really spoken to Moses from this burning bush of his. So Aaron threw down his staff and it became a snake. He put his hand in his cloak, and it came out diseased; when he put it back in, it came out healthy. We were amazed and worshiped God. With signs like that, Pharaoh couldn't possibly refuse Moses' demands.

But when I went with Moses and Aaron and the other elders of Israel to see Pharaoh, he laughed in our faces. His magicians could do all the same tricks—the snake, the diseased hand... Pharaoh not only ordered us back to work; he made us work twice as hard. A few of us thought we'd seen the snake from Aaron's staff swallow up the Egyptians' snake. Still, in a battle between our God and the Egyptian gods, it seemed like we were better off to hedge our bets.

But then the plagues started. At first it looked like a stalemate between God and the Egyptian gods. God turned the water of the Nile into blood. Pharaoh's magicians turned water to blood. God made Egypt swarm with frogs. The magicians conjured up frogs. Pharaoh was smug, and our people started complaining about Moses and his God. But I started to notice that, even though Pharaoh's gods could copy what our God was doing, not once were they able to undo any of it.

And pretty soon our God started to get the upper hand. First, he sent gnats—huge clouds of them rising up out of the dust. Then flies, in swarms so thick you couldn't see the horizon. God killed the Egyptians' livestock and their crops. He sent sickness on them and days of total darkness, and there was nothing their magicians could do. The Egyptians' gods were powerless. Osiris, the god of the Nile, couldn't cleanse his own waters. Hecate, the goddess of fertility, and Hathor, the cow goddess, couldn't save their crops or cattle. Imenhotep, god of healing, couldn't make the boils go away. And Ra, the great sun god, was obliterated from the sky. It was becoming pretty obvious to me that no god or goddess was more powerful than our God.

Not all of our people saw it that way. Even I wrestled with the question: could one God be enough? I knew that Abraham, Isaac, Jacob, and Joseph had all worshiped the One alone. Still, there *are* other powers out there. I've seen them with my own eyes. What's wrong with taking advantage of any power that can help us? But God was calling us to choose. Them or him. The many or the One. To trust that he alone is enough.

That was the question I wrestled with on the night of the Passover, the night of the firstborn, when we killed the lamb and spread its blood on our doorposts. Moses told us that God would go throughout Egypt around midnight, killing the first-born son in every family from the poorest slave right on up to Pharaoh's son. But no harm would come to any of our people whose doorways were marked with the lamb's blood.

The Egyptian gods could conjure up frogs and turn water to blood. They could make a healthy hand turn leprous, and transform a staff into a snake. But was their power enough to save us from death? Did I want to put my life, or my son's life, in the hands of lesser gods, or in the hand of the only One who seemed to have the power to save us? God wasn't offering us any middle path. In order to be saved when the angel of death passed over us, we had to walk through the blood and close our doors on sun and moon, fields and river—on everything that reminded us of the gods of Egypt.

As we stood around the table that night, sharing the bread and herbs and eating the lamb, I watched Ephraim, my son. I knew we were both thinking of the blood on the doorway, hoping—trusting—that it was enough. Deciding then and there that we would trust our God alone, no matter what anybody else did.

In the early hours of the next morning, as we left Egypt for good, Ephraim and I walked side by side past the homes of the Egyptians. From every house we heard sounds of wailing and grieving. We saw our neighbours and former masters standing hollow-eyed, clutching the bodies of their sons. Then I really saw the power of God. Shaking in my shoes, I gave thanks for his mercy and the protection he offered through the blood of a lamb.

Every time I celebrate the Passover again, it reminds me of the commitment I made—"as for me and my household, we will serve the Lord"[26]—a commitment that carried me through the wilderness, and without which I'd never have made it to this Promised Land. I've seen the power of other gods, and seen a lot of my people seduced by them. But I know that, in the end, only one God has the power to save us. And he calls us all to choose between them and him. There is no middle ground.

And so, as we get ready to share this feast—the lamb, the bread, the wine—we also get ready to consecrate ourselves again. If you haven't already, it's time to choose who you'll serve. Maybe you think God's being unfair, even closed-minded, to make us choose. But the fact is, one way or another, we each make our choice whether we realize it or not.

We're fooling ourselves if we think we can have it both ways, that we can serve the One who is all we need without actually trusting him and treating him as such. So if serving the Lord seems undesirable to you, choose for yourself right now whom you *will* serve—the gods our forefathers served in Egypt, the gods of Canaan, the gods and philosophies of your age that promise you fulfillment. But I choose to serve the only

God who can save. As for me and my household, we will serve the Lord.

Who will you serve?

17

What Will You Do With Jesus?

The Woman Caught in Adultery and the Pharisee

Scripture: John 8:2–11
Cast: 1 female, 1 male
Props: Large rock

(Enter the Pharisee, dragging a woman by the arm while she struggles and resists. He is dressed as a Pharisee; she is dishevelled, with her headscarf fallen off her head onto her shoulders. When they reach centre stage, he pushes her forward. Both turn toward the audience. He is proud and self-righteous; she looks afraid and ashamed, and avoids meeting anyone's gaze. Most of the time, they address the audience, except when they are responding to what Jesus is doing. There is a large rock centre stage.)

PHARISEE: THIS IS IT. IT'S TIME TO END THIS. FOR THE PAST WEEK, all through the Feast of Tabernacles, this Galilean has been stirring people up with his lies. He claims he's come to us from the Lord, that he can forgive sins. He heals on the Sabbath, in direct violation of Moses' command not to work on that day. Clearly he's a blasphemer. And yet he's untouchable. Even the temple guards are afraid to arrest him, because of the crowds who follow him around and hang on his every word. But now it's time to put a stop to this. To him. We can't be rid of him soon enough.

Woman: This is it. This is the end. I've been caught in the act with a man who's not my husband. I may not know much about the Law, but I know that the punishment for adultery is death. And that the Law doesn't forgive people like me. Neither will they— not the Pharisees or the priests or this rabbi they've brought me to. They're going to kill me. All I can hope for now is that they get it over with quickly.

Pharisee: He started off like all the others, just another up-start claiming to be the Messiah. We kept an eye on him but were pretty certain he'd end up like all the rest—raise a few followers, create a bit of a stir. We figured that eventually he'd go too far—denounce the Emperor or call for a revolution—and the Romans would deal with him. But then came the "miracles." Soon, bigger and bigger crowds started following him and trying to make him their king. But now it's over. He's a blasphemer, and the Law condemns him to death.

Woman: It all started off so innocently—a look, a smile, a few words. But the further things went, the riskier it got. You know how you try to fool yourself into thinking you won't get caught, but deep inside you know better? Now it's all over. I'm an adulteress, and the Law condemns me to death.

Pharisee: It's the perfect plan. See this crowd? Those soldiers on the walkway up there? The very people who kept us from arresting him over the past few days are going to be the ones who condemn him now. It's foolproof.

(Looking at the woman contemptuously, and announcing to temple crowd) This woman was found with her lover. Caught·in the act. There's no way she can deny her guilt. So we've brought her to the "great teacher" to see what he says we should do with her.

(Addressing audience) He's only got two choices, and either way he slits his own throat. Everybody here knows the Law of Moses commands us to stone her. But they also know the Romans don't allow us to carry out death sentences. If he says to stone her and incites the crowd to kill her, the Romans will arrest him as a rebel. Our hands will be clean. On the other hand, if he gives in to the Romans instead of upholding our Law, the "king" becomes a traitor. The people will turn against him— no fault of ours—and our problems will be solved. He's got no way out.

Woman: There's no way out. I'm guilty. Case closed. It's ironic—it all started out because I wanted to be loved. And now here I am, more alone than ever.

(Bitterly) Where is he, you ask? My lover? Good question. The last I saw of him, he was disappearing out the window when they *(indicating the Pharisee)* broke into the room. Funny thing is, as badly as they want to stone me, none of them seems to care about finding him. And last time I checked, it takes two to commit adultery. *(Crumpling, defeated)* Not that it matters now. I'm as good as dead. *(She lowers her head, waiting for the stones to fly.)*

Pharisee: *(Addressing Jesus, with a show of deference)* So, Rabbi, you see that this woman is guilty. What should her sentence be? *(He watches something on the ground ahead of him, surprised and bemused)* He's writing on the ground with his finger. Whatever it is, it hardly matters. He's as good as dead. *(He continues to watch intently while the woman speaks.)*

Woman: *(Briefly glancing at the spot the Pharisee is watching, then looking around)* He's writing something on the ground with his finger. I don't know what it is. I can't read it from here, but these bloodthirsty Pharisees are licking their lips. *(Watching, terrified, as the Pharisee bends down and picks up the stone)* It looks like my fate is sealed.

Pharisee: His fate is sealed. Any moment now...

Woman: ...the stones will fly.

Pharisee: *(Smugly)* And now he's looking up...

Woman: *(Fearfully)* ...and saying...

Both: *(The Pharisee with growing shock and anger, the woman with growing amazement)* "If any of you is without sin, let him throw the first stone."

Pharisee: *(Angrily)* It can't be!

Woman: *(Shocked and relieved)* It can't be!

Pharisee: How can this happen? Our plan was perfect. He knows as well as everyone else here that the woman deserves to die. Yet somehow he's turned the tables on us again! *(Sarcastically)* "If any of you is without sin..." Which one of us would be so stupid as to step forward in front of all these people and claim never to have sinned?

Woman: I can't believe it. The Pharisees look like they're ready to stone *the rabbi* now, and he just keeps calmly writing on the ground. *(Looking guardedly at the Pharisee, still unsure she's safe, wondering what he'll do.)*

(The Pharisee glares at the spot where Jesus is and clutches his rock more tightly. Then, finally, he throws the rock down. The woman winces as it hits the ground.)

Pharisee: *(Addressing audience, angrily)* This isn't over. *(He walks angrily offstage.)*

Woman: *(Looking around)* It's over. *(She looks shyly at Jesus as he stands up; she pauses while he speaks, then answers him)* There's no one left, sir. No one to condemn me.

(The woman listens, then nods gratefully and bows with her face to the ground. Then she stands, lifts her headscarf back over her head, and hurries stage left. She stops, looks over her shoulder to where Jesus was, then addresses the audience.)

Woman: I can hardly believe it. Two minutes ago, I was a dead woman. Now I'm free. I'm *free*. But what will happen to Jesus? You don't make fools of the Pharisees and priests in front of a crowd—in the temple, no less—and expect to get away with it.

I'm sure they're not finished with him. They looked like they were ready to kill him back there. Yet he took that risk for *me*. He knew I deserved to die, but he stood up for me, in front of all those people, when nobody else would. And then he said to me, "I don't condemn you, either. Go now and leave your life of sin."[27]

My "lover" abandoned me at the first sign of danger. Yet this stranger, Jesus, risked his own life to save me. What do you do when somebody gives you a gift like that? How do you thank Jesus for laying down his life to give you yours?

(The woman pauses to let the question sink in, then exits.)

About the Author

Carla Friesen-Martin has been a teacher's aide in a two-room school in Taiwan, an occupational therapist, a stay-at-home mom, and a women's Bible study leader. She currently works as a speech and language facilitator, and—best job of all—a school librarian where she gets to indulge her passion for books, reading, and sharing stories. (She hopes her students are having as much fun as she is!)

For the past twenty years, Carla has been exploring the lives of people in the Bible through writing and drama, and she has been privileged to share many of her monologues in churches, women's ministries, and retreats.

In her free time, Carla enjoys time with family and friends, traveling, reading, knitting, playing piano, kayaking, and discovering new recipes. She lives in Williams Lake, British Columbia with her family.

Endnotes

1   John 20:13.

2   John 20:13.

3   John 20:15.

4   John 20:15.

5   Psalm 23:5.

6   Jeremiah 25:15-16.

7   Matthew 26:27, Luke 22:20.

8   Matthew 20:22.

9   Matthew 20:23.

10 Luke 7:48.

11 Luke 23:34.

12 John 1:29.

13 Isaiah 53:5.

14 John 20:26.

15 John 20:27.

16 John 20:28.

17 1 Samuel 1:17.

18 1 Samuel 2:8.

19 Isaiah 41:16.

20 Matthew 3:12.

21 Luke 3:8

22 Luke 3:9.

23 Acts 9:4.

24 Acts 9:5.

25 Acts 9:5.

26 Joshua 24:15.

27 John 8:11.